Go Social, Or Go Home

7 Key Social Media

Secrets

To Get Out the Vote

and

Win Your Next

Campaign

by Dean Renfro

© 2016 by Dean Renfro
ISBN-13:
978-1533530103

ISBN-10:
1533530106

First Printing, 2016
Printed in the United States of America

Table of Contents

Disclaimer

Income Disclaimer

This book contains social media strategies, marketing methods and other advice that, regardless of my own results and experience, may not produce the same results (or any results) for you. I make absolutely no guarantee, expressed or implied, that by following the advice below you will receive votes, raise any money or improve current donations, as there are several factors and variables that come into play regarding any given campaign.

Primarily, results will depend on the nature of the campaign model, the conditions of the political climate, the experience of the individual, and situations and elements that are beyond your control.

As with any political campaign endeavor, you assume all risk related to time, energy and resource investment and money based on your own discretion and at your own potential expense.

Liability Disclaimer

By reading this book, you assume all risks associated with using the advice given below, with a full understanding that you, solely, are responsible for anything that may occur as a result of putting this information into action in any way, and regardless of your interpretation of the advice.

You further agree that our company cannot be held responsible in any way for the success or failure of your campaign as a result of the information presented in this book. It is your responsibility to conduct your own due diligence regarding the safe and successful operation of your political campaign if you intend to apply any of our information in any way to your campaign operations.

Terms of Use

You are given a non-transferable, "personal use" license to this book. You cannot distribute it or share it with other individuals.

Also, there are no resale rights or private label rights granted when purchasing this book. In other words, it's for your own personal use only.

This book has been written for information purposes only. Every effort has been made to make this book as complete and accurate as possible. However, there may be mistakes in typography or content. Also, this book provides information only up to the publishing date. Therefore, this book should be used as a guide - not as the ultimate source.

The purpose of this book is to educate. The author and the publisher does not warrant that the information contained in this book is fully complete and shall not be responsible for any errors or omissions. The author and publisher shall have neither liability nor responsibility to any person or entity with respect to any loss or damage caused or alleged to be caused directly or indirectly by this book.

Affiliate Links

The reader and user of this guide must assume that all links in this document may result in the author receiving compensation from clicking on the link.

Acknowledgements

I would like to dedicate this book to an awesome woman, my wife Lavonne. Thanks for putting up with all the ups and downs of an entrepreneurial life.

To my three kids, Dena, Joshua and Caleb my granddaughter, Makenzie and my grandson, Cayden for living through all the trials and errors and learning that "failure is not a destination."

To my mom and dad as examples of why we should all be engaged in the election process. They served as volunteers in numerous elections, served as party delegates and contributed funding, time, energy and moral support to numerous local, state and national candidates.

And to you, the reader who hopefully will take action on the ideas, questions and suggestions in this book so that the political system we honor here in the United States will produce a government by the people and for the people.

Chapter 1
Go Social, Or Go Home

Go Social, or Go Home! Those are some mighty direct words! But in today's world those words hold the power of having a campaign that is noticed, talked about and produces voter turnout versus a dismal campaign that produces minimal results, poor turnout and wasted time, energy and resources.

Whether you are an running your own campaign or have a campaign team, it is important to establish a social presence both online and with your constituents. This book is designed to provide you with some insider secrets that you need in order to establish yourself in various social media outlets that are popular today.

The main purpose of establishing yourself on social media is to provide you with more exposure. On top of that a positive social media presence can help you create creditability in your community and become the people's representative. In addition, social media provides an excellent way to engage with prospective voters. It is also a great way to engage with your current constituents, providing them with local issues, changes in policy and regulations that effect them directly, how government works and a direct connection to the political process. This type approach makes you social and positions you so that the constituents you may possibly represent will support and vote for you again and again.

This book will be your guide for building up your social media authority across the most popular social media platforms that are found today. You will learn how to create social presence that can set up the opportunity for you to make your political platform known, establish strong constituent relationships and win your campaign.

What Many People Running for Office Do Not Understand About Social Media

There are many ways that you can attract people to your website, blog, fundraiser or campaign event, but many of these ways are out of your control, except for social media. Word of mouth is a great way to gain exposure, but it is not something within your control. Social media can be controlled if you are prepared to put in some time and a little bit of effort, it is possible to build a large social media presence in a short amount of time.

Throughout this book you will discover different strategies that you can use within the most popular social media networks in order to build your social media authority and presence.

When it comes to social media there are no new fancy tricks to learn, social media is all about engendering interaction. Using social media is about compelling people consistently to engage with you and then share your content, views and opportunities. This is the main purpose of social media and it applies across every network. There is no secret formula necessary in order to become a social media success story, all you need is compelling human interaction.

What does compelling human interaction mean? Generally speaking it means that you want to involve people in a conversation that is related to your position on various matters that are important to your constituents. It is really nothing more complicated than this.

The key to social media is being social. By pure definition, social media should be a two-way street. If someone is commenting on your posts, take the time to comment back. You should be having conversations with the people who are following you, who attend your rallies, come to your campaign speeches, who write or call.

Many social media enthusiasts are simply obsessed with the online interaction. The number of followers or likes that they get on their posts as much as they are with the amount of traffic their website or blog receives. In reality, these numbers do not have much to do with the true metrics of being successful with social media.

Instead of focusing solely on the number of new likes that you get on some social online media platform, you should focus on the number of people who are commenting on and then sharing your content online and offline. The number who engage with you in a conversation at a rally, who take time to write you or call you to discuss a matter or position - This is the true measure of engagement. When more people are engaging with your content and dialogue the more likely they are to share it, which will increase your exposure and spread your message.

Building Your Social Profile

As mentioned before, and as will be discussed in further detail in later chapters, the best way to build your social profile is to create compelling presence and value based content on a consistent basis. However, this is not going to build an audience. If no one is reading your content or attending your rallies, then no one is going to be sharing them and spreading the news about you.

To get the best leverage through social presence and media you will need to get to the point where the number of followers that you have is enough to provide you with growth through sharing. Getting to this point is easier said than done.

In the next chapters we will look at key insider secrets and action steps to take on each of the social media outlets in order to improve your social media authority for your campaign. So roll up your sleeves and Go Social, or Go Home!

Chapter 2
Social Media Is Not Just Technology

Well if it's not about technology – what is about then? Great question! While much of what exist today in social media and technology – five years ago, didn't exist. Five years from now – it will be different. Shoot it may change drastically tomorrow – technology doesn't happen through a series of little steps, it usually is more like leaps and bounds.

But one thing hasn't changed for centuries – social networking. Technology is just a tool, interaction and engagement between people still lie at the core of "social media." It also is the key to a winning political campaign. If you are thinking that somehow you can wave the social media magic wand and you will win –

you might need to rethink the political campaign concept.

Social Media is just what is says it is, but it is often viewed from the eyes of technology. With the rise of social platforms like Facebook, Twitter, LinkedIn, Instagram, Snapchat and a whole host of others, it would be easy to understand how that would be the thinking. But at the core of each of these platforms is the engagement of real people. People with common likes, similar stages of life, sameness of cultures, on and on.

So let's define Social media. The social part of the term is commonly seen in light of communities of people connected, sharing information, ideas, communication, common interest, traditions, language among a group of people. The engagement among these commonalities create a bond, a cohesiveness, a tribe, a niche, even a culture. The power of people to engage with one another make up the social aspect of social media.

In turn add the word media, to social and you have a tool for communication, a platform where all these elements can be expressed. From early on, man as sought various mediums to share what he/she knows with others. Written and spoken language, sign language, music, art, symbols, and now technology.

So as a candidate you must remember at the core of all this is connecting with a network of people, through various mediums. These mediums are vast and more are developing and being released each day, it seems. So find what works best between you and your constituents and leverage it to get out the votes and win an election.

Chapter 3
Key Secret Number 1
It's All About KLT

What's with the initials? Is some secret code? Not really, but it makes for a shorter title! It stands for Know, Like Trust. Networking and referral expert Bob Burg is famous for his quote (from the excellent book "Endless Referrals"): **"All things being equal, people do business with, and refer business to people they know, like and trust."**

While it may on the surface make common sense, people often never enact this simple concept. When I talk about the know factor it carries more than just the answer to the question, "Do you know him/her?" It's really all about the whole – life, interest, thinking, positions, activities about you. When your name is called or mentioned people feel comfortable enough to identify with you. This first step will up to you, how far you can comfortably go. Being transparent, real, authentic is difficult for many. But the more quickly you can be identified as someone who is like us, the quicker you can be seen as "someone I know."

On the heel of that is the like factor. Being seen as likable is key. People have difficulty doing much of anything with someone they don't "like." Being likeable comes by being authenticate, some who they would identify with, connect to. Likeability can be effected by how one looks and or sounds. The perception of who you are creates a certain likeability factor.

Trust is created when someone delivers on what they say or promise. It could be tied to being consistent, or approachable or even open.

None of this happens overnight. It may take several times of meeting you, hearing you and observing your person, attitude, tone, conversation and actions before you experience KLT. But in the end, without you will not get far. With it, you have a golden ticket.

Chapter 4
Key Secret Number 2
This Principle Rules
Use It

Use the 80/20 rule in social media! It's one thing to socialize and another to self-promote on social media. The biggest turn off is over-the-top self-promotion. Your audience can smell it from a mile away. If you keep pushing yourself and promoting yourself on social media, you'll lose followers and ultimately hurt your identity and the campaign.

So what can you do so that you can continue promoting and at the same time retain your followers? By using the 80/20 principle! The practice is simple - focus on the 20% that gives you 80% of the results.

In social media, what you want to do is use this rule for the following:
80% should be about your audience.
20% self-promotion.

So 80% should be about helping your audience and making your posts about THEM. A conservative 20% can be about you and your campaign and promotions about your campaign. Stick by this rule and you'll have happy followers and constituents!

The 80/20 of Social Media

So using this principle how does a person running for a political office use it, you ask? Great question! Here's some ideas to help.

- If you run ads on Facebook, let 80% of your ads be about the issues, positions, and what matters to constituents that support your positions. Why? Because the more agreement you can create between you and them, the more support and sharing they will do.

- Your postings on Facebook, Twitter, LinkedIn, Instagram, your Blog and even Snap-Chat should also utilize the 80-20 principle. Post about what the issues are, what your position is, key elements that your potential voter wants to hear about.

- When you are out in the field among the voters, spend 80% of your time getting input from your constituents. Ask them questions, seek their insights, feel their pain, hear what matters to them. Most people aren't looking for you to change your position, they just want to know they were heard. Have someone responsible to gather names and numbers from those who give input, answer questions, voice concerns – then contact them and thank them. You can do that through mailing a personal card, like SendOutCards. Or you could use a service that leaves a voice message on their cell phone. It's not a Robo-Call, but a service that leaves a message on their cell phone without ringing their phone. Like in the old days of AOL, "You have mail" and every one rushed to see their email – because it was so rare in those days, the person's phone notifies them they have a voicemail! What do you suppose they do? What do you suppose they think? How about comments like, "Wow – candidate so and so actually called me and left me a message thanking me for sharing." Do you suppose they might tell a few people about that?

Today's technology has advanced so far and fast many candidates and campaign managers aren't aware of all the new opportunities. Whether it's live streams like Periscope, Facebook Live, SnapChat, Twitter and Instagram Videos, or Ringless Voice Mail, or Retargeting, or "Alerts" or Video Emails. If you aren't in that field, you won't know all the new tools that could help you get out the vote and win your campaign.

But the smart candidate will realize that having an expert social media manager will give him/her an unfair advantage, an advantage that positions him/her for winning the campaign.

Chapter 5
Key Secret Number 3
REV Your Campaign

The concept of "social" media is all about being social and having social engagement. Too often would be candidates, as well as, seasoned incumbents get caught up in the hype of the campaign. They often lose sight of the big picture – representing their constituents.

Injecting our third key secret can propel a candidate ahead quickly. Using the REV approach, the candidate can quickly build a relationship with the constituents, educate them about key issues and then offer value to them.

Relationship building is at the core of social media. The whole premise of Facebook is built on the idea of relationships. The "Fan" page, the "Like" and "Share" buttons are all activities that people with relationships do. Granted it has been exploited and over used, but it still remains a valid component of relationship.

When you post a comment, a story, a picture, and even a video the idea is to create engagement. To incite a conversation with people who have a relationship. If you research a post that has numerous comments, you will often see that those posting the comments have and obvious relationship with each other.

What better way than for a candidate to engage in similar activity. Using information post, inquiry post, polls and quizzes candidates can quickly start a relationship engagement. Again this is all a part of being the candidate that is connected, listening, cares about the people. The old adage, "People don't a care how much you know, until they know how much you care."

A sharp social media manager can create this kind of relationship building with numerous tools that schedule post, automate post response, use "alerts" that track comments, lead capture for building an email list to create an ongoing process to educate the constituents, split test ads, video responses to comments, live candidate and constituent interviews.

Educating your audience is a process. One mail piece, one stump speech, one yard sign, one conversation is not going to convince nor educate most people enough to create "raging" fans who will be your "in the field" evangelist. The more of those you have, the easier it is to win the election.

Educating your audience can be a rather simple process using technology. Much of what will be shared in your campaign can be repurposed if you make plans. Again a sharp social media manager can help you plan out how to do that. Creating a connected series of emails, a series of videos, a sequenced set of speeches or talks that are also recorded and then merged with slide show presentations that can be used on a website, video channels – like YouTube, Vimeo, Dailymotion, Facebook, LinkedIn, Twitter, Instagram and Snapchat to name a few (there are many more).

Delivering value is another vital role that social media plays in helping you position you as the candidate of choice. Using social media you are able to repetitively deliver value – "I hear you," "I have a solution," "You spoke, I listened, Let's do this together," all communicate a very important value that people are looking for: my voice and vote matter!

Three simple pieces of information is all it takes to really give you the unfair advantage over your opponents if you use the right tools and build your campaign on the REV secret. I talk more about that in the last chapter.

Chapter 6
Key Secret Number 4
Story Tellers Get the Votes

In the land of distracted and message bombarded constituents – the storytelling candidate will win. The more stories you can tell, the more your constituents will listen and share. Storytelling is as old as mankind. We have been telling and listening to stories our whole lives. The candidate who taps into this secret and does it well and often will have an unfair advantage over the other candidates in the race.

Social media is a storyteller's heaven. Used correctly and often your stories will spread. A knowledgeable social media manage that understands the power of story can help you put your story out there in a variety of forms and mediums. Whether it's a Facebook Live video that is shot with local constituents, an interview with a local business person, a "meet my newest supporter" video, an email sequence that tells the story over a series of emails, a strategic stump speech or a door-to-door "I wanted to meet you and hear what you have to say" neighborhood walk – all are fonder for stories.

But there's a secret here – it's not just about the story – it's about how you use the story! Stories have to be positioned to have the most power. Having a plethora of stories makes that easy. It really then leverages the 80/20 principle and helps build the Know, Like and Trust factor because most of the conversation is not about you – it's about them.

Chapter 7
Key Secret Number 5
Leveraging WIIFU

One of the first things that people tend to talk about is "WIIFM" "what's in it for me?" For a new candidate or even an incumbent, that could really come across as arrogant, or egotistical, or singular focused. So the solution is to turn to "what's in it for us?" That formula allows you to create a dialogue and find out what questions and concerns your constituents want answered or solved. Having this dialogue builds your presence, your ideas, your cause. Building a common cause allows people to move past minor issues and rally about a bigger concern.

Social Media fits that solution to a "t." It allows you to connect directly to constituents, create numerous threads of conversations, build ideas and create a common cause. With Facebook's massive data collection, you can pinpoint people in your voting area by all kinds of data. This allows you to have a pulse on how to "talk" to them, gather them into like-minded groups and have a conversation with them.

Using this data coupled with technology you can customize your message in your emails, in video, in live streams, in tweets, even in graphics in Instagram. Never before has a candidate had such power to reach out and touch the constituents.

Not only can you create a common cause, you can connect people to the cause by customizing how they can contribute to your campaign. Imagine knowing the buying habits of people, know if they shop online, buy online, what credit cards they use, what their preferences are about numerous issues

Chapter 8
Key Secret Number 6
You – Everywhere - Now

In the old school philosophy of political campaigning, contributions were "king." Meaning that the candidate with the most money was most likely to win. Often this was because of the sheer power of being able to have more direct mail pieces, a larger billboard, more radio or TV time, or more yard signs and bumper stickers. While all those certainly play a big role, and deep pockets are important, a new player on the block – social media – has leveled the playing field.

With social media and the tools connected to it, you can personally reach out and touch people with a personal message, with a directed action, with a constant presence, with

an appearance of, "you, everywhere, now."
The concept behind this is driven by the power
of social media. You can be totally unknown
and suddenly appear on the scene as a
"breath of fresh air." You can be everywhere
people go, whether it's to drop off the kids at
school, shopping at the local grocery store or
attend a local event – you can be noticed.

With the power of retargeting (you may not
even know that that is – but it's ok – a sharp
social media manager does) you can follow
people all over social media and the internet.
You can "show up" wherever they go. It's like
you are everywhere! Couple that with new
beacon technology that can drop a message in
your constituent's smartphone when they
come in range of the beacon that has been
strategically placed – you show up! Follow that
up with a ringless voice message and you are
suddenly top of mind. Schedule another

ringless voice message to follow up your direct mail piece with a personal message like, "Sorry I missed you, I sent you a post card, you should have gotten it in the last couple of days. Your opinion is important to me, so if you have any concerns or questions, call me back at xxx-xxx-xxxx. I want to hear from you."

Connect this together with a social media ad campaign that points out the same message – you are suddenly everywhere now! People start to feel like they know you. They feel like you have their best interest in mind, they feel like you know their concerns! The perception becomes that you have your hand on everything. That you know the heartbeat of the issues, that you're connected to everyone they know. Part of this secret is being able to go the neighborhoods and connect face to face with people and talk about their issues. How

do you do that? Check the closing chapter –
I'll tell you how.

Chapter 9
Key Secret Number 7
The Secret Sauce Works
Every Time

The secret may seem counterintuitive to some. Many times the approach taught is find out what works and model that. And that is true. Often you can model that and it works. But in a political campaign one other secret can set you apart in a race. That secret is to find out what everyone else is doing and do the opposite. If all the other candidates are putting out yard signs and billboards, by all means put some out, but spend your time, knocking on doors, shaking hands and as the old saying goes, kissing babies. Visit civic meetings, churches, local events, make personal phone calls, put yourself as much as possible toe to toe with your constituents.

Another component to this secret is to make sure that you follow up and follow through. Every meeting and every person is another opportunity to connect. Get a system in place that allows you to gather data: names, phone numbers, email address. These can prove the difference in getting the vote out and winning the election.

Conclusion

By now you have realized that social media is something that can be quite overwhelming to someone who participates in it on a casual basis. It can be the difference maker in your campaign. The ability to connect with people of all ages, professions, economic levels and interest is the primary key in setting yourself up to win and election. It creates the basis for contributions, for connections, and for networks of people who will volunteer to help you in your campaign.

Never before have candidates had some much connectivity power as they have today with social media. So you need to seek out a competent social media manager. Someone who knows what tools are available. Someone who understands the importance of social networking, someone who can help you be social or else you might be going home before it all gets started.

Contact me for a free 30 minute consultation to see how we might work together to help you get out the vote and win your election.

You can contact me by booking a time to discuss this at https://deanrenfro.youcanbook.me/

Talk with you soon.